Harriet's Book

Fewer, Shorter, Better Meetings

D1741249

Rowmark

Other Easy Step by Step Guides in the series include:

Telemarketing, Cold Calling & Appointment Making

Marketing

Building a Positive Media Profile

Stress and Time Management

Motivating Your Staff

Recruiting the Right Staff

Better Budgeting for your Business

Writing Advertising Copy

Writing Articles and Newsletters

Managing Change

Handling Confrontation

Being Positive and Staying Positive

Giving Confident Presentations

Successful Selling

Communicating With More Confidence

Fundraising For Your School

All the above guides are available from:
Rowmark Limited
65 Rogers Mead
Hayling Island
Hampshire
England PO11 0PL

Telephone: 023 9246 1931
Fax: 023 9246 0574
E mail: enquiries@rowmark.co.uk
www.rowmark.co.uk

Easy Step by Step Guide

Fewer, Shorter, Better Meetings

Brian Lomas

Rowmark

Published by Rowmark Limited
65 Rogers Mead
Hayling Island
Hampshire
England
PO11 0PL

ISBN 0 9539856 8 7

Typeset by Freelance Publishing Services, Brinscall, Lancs
Printed in Great Britain by RPM Reprographics Ltd. Chichester.

Contents

About the author

Brian Lomas is a trainer, business consultant, part-time lecturer and managing director based on the south coast of England. He has worked in Britain and the United States for different types of companies – from established multinationals to two-person start-up companies. All of these organizations had one common drain on productivity – too many meetings which go on for too long and perhaps fail to achieve any progress.

So this guide is an accumulation of his – and many others' – past experiences coupled with a desire – nay, a passion! – to get much more out of life and work by having fewer, shorter, better meetings.

For Christine

Introduction

There are some meetings that are never supposed to be managed or to be that effective – sometimes we should just be getting together or perhaps 'putting the world to rights'. As a highly social and communicative species, it would be too robotic to live our lives without some chit-chat or gossip. Sometimes, it's just great to be human!

But there are meetings which could be better planned, better managed or shorter – if they have to be scheduled at all. At such times, it's vital to have a set of tools and techniques which can be used to make the difference – and that is what this guide seeks to give you, its readers.

You can use this guide to improve the vast array of meetings that could be called – be it team briefings, training sessions, reviewing and improving performance, making decisions or planning for the future – to list just a few. This guide will work for you because all effective meetings have common themes – they have structure, a chosen style, preparation and planning and all serve one goal – to achieve a purpose effectively.

How to use this guide

As is now standard with an easy step by step guide, you can use it in multiple ways – dip in and out of the summaries or 'boxed' text, read it cover to cover or find the one aspect of meetings you would like to improve within the contents section.

Whatever your approach, take special note of this message:

You don't have to be 'in charge' to improve a meeting. You don't even have to be in charge to abolish it.

But you do have to follow the guide!

What you will learn from this guide

- How to identify meetings which could be scrapped

- How alternatives to meetings can be more effective

- How to plan and prepare effectively for a meeting

- How to define a meeting's purpose and develop an agenda

- How to decide who should attend

- How roles within meetings differ but responsibilities are shared by all

- How to determine the best timing and location of meetings

- How to get meetings off to the right start

- How to get difficult messages across at meetings

- How to encourage and manage conflict in meetings

- How to analyze problems and achieve decisions through meetings

- How to follow up on meetings

- How to assess whether or not a meeting was worth it.

1

So why do we meet?

We meet for a variety of reasons. Here are just some of them:

- to think creatively, generate ideas

- to gather, share and/or evaluate experiences, information, thoughts or opinions

- to create cohesion and/or clarity of understanding

- to analyse a problem and identify its cause(s)

- to discuss and then make a decision or agreement

- to negotiate

- to resolve disputes

- to respond to an issue which is or has become too complex to deal with in any other way

- to develop/implement a plan

- to co-ordinate or delegate activity

- to assess progress/performance and take any consequent action

- to seek or give support/advice

- to interview or appraise

- to train, coach or instruct

- to discipline, punish, reward or praise (praise in front of others is good, criticism is preferable in private)

- to achieve 'soft' benefits (team building, motivation, caring, inspiration, commitment, mutual support, attitudinal/behavioural understanding etc)

- to create change

- to deliver a single, consistent message to a wide audience at exactly the same time

- to fulfill legal requirements (e.g. an Annual General Meeting).

However, even if listed above, it does not mean that a meeting is the best means of fulfilling that purpose.

To know whether or not a meeting is the best way to address an issue, perhaps we should start by defining what a meeting actually is …

What is a meeting?

A meeting is 'a gathering of more than one person for a specific purpose'.

Two friends might 'meet' in the supermarket. A conversation ensues although without any real purpose in mind. It therefore falls outside of our definition. (How would your friend react if you started a conversation in the supermarket by asking what the specific purpose of your conversation was going to be?)

The word 'gathering' is also important to our definition. If two people 'gather' in different rooms linked by video conferencing, there can still be a meeting. Therefore:

A 'gathering' does not necessarily mean meeting in a single location.

Too many meetings!

Have you ever heard – or thought – any of the following?

'I haven't done any work today – I've been stuck in

meetings'

'He isn't available right now – he's in a meeting. I have no idea how long it is going to last'

'I'm really not sure what was decided during the last meeting'

'Meetings give me a break from the telephone'

'The last meeting? Well, the coffee and doughnuts were worth going for!'

'I don't know why I bother going to such meetings – my opinion doesn't seem to make any difference'

'Meetings rival watching paint dry for boredom'

'If I have to listen to them rambling/ranting on any more, I will ... '

Whatever your perception of meetings, one thing we can all probably say is that we have had some bad experiences. So when you are asked to a meeting – or thinking of calling one – perhaps you should ask:

Is this meeting really necessary?

Will it add value for all concerned?

Let's look at these questions in more detail.

Is the meeting necessary?

There are four criteria which make a meeting necessary – or not. First:

> **Meet if the communication *needs* to be two-way.**

Now this should be the perception of both parties' needs. So a manager may think that declaring a number of redundancies is a one-way communication, but those impacted will need the opportunity to ask questions and seek clarification. So a meeting is essential in this case. (Although perhaps not immediately because people will need time to absorb the information and think of possible questions).

Two-way communication can still, however, be achieved through the written word. So we add a second criteria for validating that a meeting is necessary:

> **Meet if people need to interreact.**

For instance, if there is a need to 'bounce' ideas around a group of people.

And our third criteria for determining whether or not a meeting might be necessary:

> **Meet if everyone needs to know something at the same time.**

For instance, a travel company that was de-merging from another arranged meetings across its entire operation at the same time (even taking account of different time zones) to ensure all its employees were told the same thing at exactly the same time. They even made arrangements to communicate with those absent from work at the appointed time.

And our fourth – and final – criteria for determining whether or not there needs to be a meeting:

> **Meet if it is the only way to fulfill the sensory need.**

Now that sounds a bit wordy – let's see if we can simplify it a bit with a few examples:

If I want to know what you think of tinned salmon – a questionnaire might suffice: you can open the tin and it should be as consistent as any other tin of salmon. But if I want to know what you think about my new recipe for fresh salmon poached in white wine, we need to meet – I need to ensure that it is perfectly cooked before you sample it. It is a question of degree that the relevant senses – those of taste and smell – need to be fulfilled.

Another example would be that we don't need to 'meet' to listen to Elvis Presley – just listen to one of his recordings. And if you want to 'see' him sing, a DVD or video is fine. But ask anyone who ever attended one of his live performances and they will say it was much more stimulating than sitting at home with a recording – they got a lot more from it by going to a 'meeting'. So:

> **The greater the degree of sensual stimulation needed, the greater the need for a meeting.**

This last criteria also disbars telephone calls from our definition of a meeting – if all we need to do is hear another speak, a call might be fine. However, if we also need to *see* their body language and reactions, a meeting is required.

The five human senses (some hold that there are six) are taste, smell, sight, sound and touch. I am no expert on the sixth sense, but the gist is that there is more to it than the five alone – there is, Extra Sensory Perception. You get a 'feeling' about other people in a meeting which a telephone call cannot reveal.

To utilize the above points effectively in securing **fewer** meetings:

> Challenge the calling of any meeting which fails to meet any of the four criteria which determine its necessity.

And we can make a further challenge to reduce the number of meetings – a meeting should 'add value' for all concerned. Adding value might refer to either 'hard' or 'soft' benefits.

Hard benefits and adding value

Hard benefits are the financial gain that will be achieved as a result of a meeting.

For example: if a meeting takes place to negotiate the sale of a piece of equipment, the benefit for the supplier would be the profit made and for the purchaser, the benefit might be the productivity gains and cost savings that the equipment will generate.

But it is not quite that simple!

If a supplier flies three executives 500 miles to conduct this negotiation, provides them with overnight accommodation and meals, all of the costs need to be taken into account. So we calculate:

- What is the cost of employing three executives for a day? (The amount of time they will probably be away from their other work). And 'costs' here means more than just the salaries. It includes things like the employer's pension or tax costs and the cost of creating the role – office space, computer equipment etc. Try doubling an annual salary to get an idea of the cost of employing people.

Plus:

- the travel and subsistence costs for these three people to travel and stay overnight

and

- the profit they will *not* earn as a result of being away from their place of work for a day.

Is the supplier still going to make profit from the sale of the piece of equipment? Perhaps such a meeting is now failing to add any value.

And, of course, the buyer's company must also calculate whether their gain will also be positive from attending a meeting. So before agreeing to meet, ask:

> **Is this meeting going to add hard benefits for everyone?**

Soft benefits and adding value

Even if there is no hard benefit, we might still meet when the 'soft' (or intangible) benefits are deemed to be worth it. Soft benefits include:

- **team building**: it is difficult to feel part of a team when you have never met the others involved

- **motivation**: it is hard to inspire people by giving them a few words on a piece of paper

- **caring**: it is difficult to show how much you care if you aren't prepared to meet with someone. (Try asking elderly relatives who live apart from you whether or not a telephone call suffices).

In business, we could perhaps work these soft benefits into some form of financial gain. For example: a more motivated workforce is a more productive workforce. But it is not always possible to demonstrate a financial gain – how could you put a price on showing someone you care? So a meeting may be appropriate, even when financially detrimental, if the 'soft benefits' are significant.

Think about the consequences of not meeting

A quick and easy way to challenge whether or not a meeting should be held is to ask what would be the consequences if the meeting was not held. The less serious the consequences, the less appropriate a meeting would be.

Think about the consequences of meeting

This was partly considered when we discussed the work that would not be done because people were in a meeting – the potential lost opportunities incurred because people are absent from their 'normal' work. However, there is another important aspect to consider which might prevent a meeting from taking place:

> If a meeting would endanger confidentiality or security, perhaps it should not be held.

For example: a retailer could not hold a marketing strategy meeting because one of the attendees was releasing information to her best friend who worked for a competitor. So the strategy was determined outside of a meeting – unless, that is, they sought to 'leak' information to the competitor!

'Rubber-stamp' meetings

It is always worth checking whether or not the purpose of a meeting is a fabrication – a way of window-dressing:

> Is this meeting merely giving the appearance of adding value?

For example, I have witnessed:

- a manager who wanted to create the illusion of consultation and/or participation – but had no intention of allowing any comment to influence his decision

- a department head who wanted to share/pass the responsibility and blame over a failed initiative

- the chief executive who wanted to enhance his ego, profile and power.

Typically, such motives for calling a meeting would rarely become apparent until it has started – but don't just sit there! Check your understanding of the purpose.

The alternatives

So having identified all sorts of reasons why meetings should *not* take place, let's consider some of the alternatives:

- **do nothing**: perhaps a bit drastic, but if a meeting is not justifiable, it might be better not to call a meeting or to decline the invitation to attend one

- do something to **add greater value**: are you really going to be condemned for tripling the year's profits instead of attending a meeting?

- **make a telephone call**: there's still some cost, but at least the travel costs are avoided and it would be more time efficient

- **write a letter, fax or e-mail** if the aim is merely to pass on information

- **Use a web-based discussion** room/board to enable an exchange of ideas or questions. It may not be quite as personal, but it does allow people to sign in and out at their convenience.

> In short, never arrange, nor attend, a meeting unless there is going to be added value as a result.

But if a meeting has to take place ...

Consider the following options:

- attend only the part of the meeting relevant to you

- minimize your travel costs by having an 'electronic' meeting, a video conference. See Chapter 5 for more on this

- send a representative with the necessary authority to act and speak on your behalf

- shorten a meeting's duration by having relevant information circulated in advance (a sound principle for all meetings)

- send a report and don't attend – although there may be questions arising which you will not be available to answer and, of course, your report could be rejected in your absence

- request a copy of the minutes or action points from the meeting rather than attend.

Meetings – the positive

Having spent most of this chapter trying to talk you out of meetings, perhaps I should just summarize the positive aspects of meetings – or, more precisely, the positive aspects of effective meetings, which:

- achieve more by attendees coming together than by working alone (a key reason for all meetings)

- deliver added value – in hard financial terms and/ or soft benefits

- are quicker and more efficient than some of the alternatives

- create involvement and commitment

In summary

- a meeting is 'a gathering of more than one person for a specific purpose' – but it is not necessary to meet in the same location

- there are lots of good reasons to meet – but there are many occasions when one of the alternatives is sufficient

- meet if there is a need for two-way communication, for interaction between participants, for everyone to know something at the same time and/or for sensory stimulation

- consider whether or not a potential meeting will

add value for all concerned, be it hard (financial gain) or soft (intangible) benefits

- think about the possible consequences both of meeting and of not meeting, before determining whether or not a meeting is appropriate

- be certain that there is real purpose in a meeting – it is not just window-dressing or a rubber stamp

- consider the alternatives to a meeting before scheduling or agreeing to attend one

- effective meetings can be highly positive experiences.

2

Setting a meeting's purpose

We have already defined a meeting as 'a gathering of more than one person for a specific purpose'. So, having decided to have a meeting, our preparation starts with how to develop that purpose. We do this by asking:

> What am I seeking to achieve?
> Why is this meeting being called?
> What would make it a success?

What am I seeking to achieve?

Whether you are the meeting's organizer or an invitee, this question should always be asked. There is no point to a meeting unless there is clarity about what it seeks to achieve. For example:

Greater mutual support within the team.

Why is this meeting being called?

This question may – or may not – give the same answer as the first – it is always worth checking! For example:

'There have been three specific instances in the last week when a failure in team working has damaged our customer relationships and they need to be resolved.'

What would make it successful?

This should connect the above answers to the added value (be it in hard or soft benefits) which derive from the meeting. To continue with the example:

'There will be an immediate reduction in the number of complaints from customers in relationship to the service they receive.'

So the success criteria might not always be apparent at the end of the meeting itself – it may take time for effective monitoring to identify that success.

Defining the purpose

Now we have the answers to the three questions, we can define the purpose of the meeting. For example:

'The purpose of this meeting is to ensure that our customers' perceptions of our service are increasingly positive, not least by analyzing where past failures have occurred and determining an appropriate action

to prevent any future reoccurrence.'

A poor purpose would be:

'To analyze past customer complaints and make sure the boss finds a scapegoat.'

We could sum up this latter 'purpose' as 'passing the buck' – and therefore, a meeting should never be called.

Is the purpose reasonable?

It's worth checking! Don't set the meeting up for failure before it has even started. Check in advance with the attendees that they believe – as you should – that it is reasonable. An example of unreasonableness:

'The purpose of the meeting is to ensure that no customer ever complains about our service ever again.'

Alas, however good an ideal it may be, it is unworkable as long as you have customers.

The time gap between arranging a meeting and it taking place can have a profound effect on a meeting's purpose:

> If the purpose is no longer valid or reasonable by the time the meeting is scheduled to be held, cancel it.

Further, if new information comes to light, which impacts the purpose or its achievement:

> To adjourn is better than stumbling through a meeting ill-prepared.

Multiple purposes

There is nothing inherently wrong with a meeting having more than one purpose providing the approach outlined above is followed for each point. However, there are dangers.

Long meetings tire people and the effort put in to achieve a purpose discussed later in the meeting can be less than for one at the top of the agenda. Sometimes people will stop discussing a point and/or acquiesce just to escape the meeting room; at other times they may disagree with an issue merely because they feel that they wrongly lost an earlier debate.

People can struggle in meetings if they suddenly have to 'change tack'. Perhaps their input is required on one item and they are expected to simply listen to the next – but their inclination will be to carry on offering input (see Chapter 3).

Set a date

The obvious principle here is:

> Never set a date too late to fulfill the purpose(s).

This can be difficult: I once tried to schedule a meeting with six people. We discounted the days of the week which would conflict with their business demands and priorities, then looked for an available date. When we failed to find a date in the following three months, alarm bells rang!

It turned out that people were accepting diary dates for meetings before their purpose was known. Ironically, the meeting I was seeking to schedule was to train participants in better time management!

If a date cannot be readily agreed, ask:

- do the would-be attendees see a benefit from attending?' (See 'motivating attendance' in Chapter 3)

- have participants challenged the filling of their diaries with other meetings? Do they add value? Have they real purpose?

- does everyone have a clear understanding of their own (and their organization's) priorities?

- does each person understand the essential need for their presence in achieving the purpose?

- has the agenda been published and agreed?

So, setting a date may be difficult – people go on holiday and have other commitments. If, however, the above points are checked, it should be easier.

I can't resist stating something particularly irritating about 'regular' meetings – those called once a week, month or whatever. Such are usually scheduled without agendas. So how can it be known that it is an effective use of time? Yes, team building and other 'soft benefits' (see Chapter 1) can be anticipated but – and it's a big 'but' – has the purpose been agreed before the date is scheduled?

> Regularly scheduled meetings should always be challenged.

Publicize the purpose and date

Before publicizing the purpose and date, check whether or not a meeting is appropriate (see Chapter 1). If a meeting is the answer, give enough notice for everyone to have the time to prepare.

Note that participants may be on holiday and/or busy with other work so do not assume that they can prepare immediately on receipt of the agenda. Conversely, if you send an agenda out too early, it may be put to one side and then forgotten about.

If appropriate, distribute a location map with directions. Not everyone may have their own transport available – so public transport information and the potential for car-share could be given.

Check in advance that everyone will be ready for the meeting (and has not forgotten about it!)

A question of style

Having established the necessity for and the purpose(s) of a meeting, you can now look at the appropriate style – the way or manner that the meeting is to be conducted.

> The style of the meeting will impact the achievement of its purpose.

There are two style extremes – formal and informal. Some meetings may reflect one of these styles – for instance an Annual General Meeting will be highly formalized. Yet team building meetings with total informality are unlikely to achieve their purpose – so there are many styles between the two extremes.

Let's look at some illustrations of different styles:

- the chairperson may require everyone to address comments 'through the chair'. This is highly controlling and can therefore stilt the flow and openness during the meeting – but it is more likely to stay within the allotted time

- a 'fun' approach can help creative thinking – from playing with toys to giving everyone a box of crayons

- a large group (which can quickly get out of control) will need more formality than a small one

- if disciplining a member of staff, a serious tone will have to be established and maintained

- a 'top' table or stage would destroy any perception of everyone being equal – something that could be done with a circle of chairs with everyone on the same level

- the culture of an organization may require, for instance, that no meeting lasts longer than fifteen minutes. Such meetings would be very different in style to that of an all-day meeting

- the culture of participants may require that certain etiquettes are strictly adhered to as part of the meeting style.

So the purpose, number of participants and culture will influence the appropriate style.

In summary

- always start preparing for a meeting – whether calling or attending it – by establishing its purpose – and checking it is reasonable

- a purpose is developed by asking what it seeks to achieve, why is it being called and what would have happened to make it a success?

- cancel a meeting if its purpose becomes invalid or unreasonable

- adjourn a meeting if more preparation time is needed because of changing circumstances or information

- challenge any regularly scheduled meeting for purpose and value added

- set a date that is not too late to fulfill the purpose

- if there is particular difficulty in agreeing dates, re-assess whether or not there is a clarity of understanding about the meeting's purpose, priority, benefit, value added and the participants' roles

- publicize the purpose and date to enable everyone to prepare properly

- meetings can have more than one purpose, but it can be difficult for people to change from one issue to another

- the style of a meeting needs to be determined, taking into account its purpose, number of participants and culture of those involved.

3
Who should attend?

Now we have the purpose and style worked out, we can identify who needs to be at the meeting.

To achieve your purpose, you will need those who:

- have relevant specialist knowledge/input

- are likely to be impacted by the outcomes expected from the meeting

- hold or have authority over key resources that might be needed to achieve the purpose and deliver its outcomes

- are representative of any of the above (providing they have the necessary knowledge, skill and power to act)

- have a specific role to play in the meeting – for instance, as facilitator.

Consider also whether or not it is safe to exclude:

- those who have strong negative opinions about an agenda item
- those who have the potential to disrupt/wreck the purpose and outcomes beyond the meeting
- those who are advocates of the purpose and may be needed to counterbalance anticipated negativity from others.

It may appear to be the easy option to exclude those opposed to the meeting's purpose, but this could be a big mistake!

Here's an example: I was invited to a meeting whose purpose was to organize the content of a company's national conference. I agreed with the purpose and required outcomes from the conference, but, at the first meeting, vehemently (perhaps too vehemently) opposed the recommended approach. Some weeks passed and I registered my concern that no further meetings had been called and I was told: 'Oh they are meeting, they just decided it was better if you weren't invited.'

I could then have become a highly disruptive influence – all the more so when they came to me and asked me to make a speech at the conference. But I 'bit my lip', kept quiet and made the speech.

The point is that I *could* have become highly disruptive, yet I also *could* have become a useful sounding board for the meeting to reach the best possible decision. As it happens, I failed in my role because I did not communicate my concerns in an acceptable way. (A key learning point for me.) Yet the meeting organizers should not have excluded me just because they didn't like what I said (or even the way I said it).

Who should not attend?

Exclude anyone who has nothing to offer the purpose or achievement of the outcomes. Just because someone has always been invited to a regular meeting, it doesn't mean they should be there. Nor does it mean they want to be there!

Consider part-time attendance

If someone's input is not required for the whole meeting, why ask them to sit there and waste their time? An agenda can be constructed to allow 'visiting participants' to attend at specific times for individual subjects – providing you keep to your agenda timetable!

Motivating attendance

We start by ensuring everyone knows all the necessary details: When should they be where – and for how long? What is the agenda they must prepare for? Why have they been invited? However:

> Providing details is one thing – motivating attendance and participation is quite another.

Give them a 'what's in it for me? – a **WIIFM?** For example:

If I asked everyone in your organization to stay behind

after work for five hours (without pay!) so that we could increase the profit/surplus by 5%, how many would say 'Of course, no problem"?

I suspect there wouldn't be too many volunteers because although the organization and principal stakeholders might gain something, many others in the organization would not see any benefit for themselves. So to motivate their attendance, I would need a WIIFM? for each person – perhaps time off in lieu or perhaps 'We may need to substantially cut costs, but we need your input to ensure that it will have the least negative impact on your team's morale.' This should get them thinking and ensure their attendance and fullest participation.

Non-attendance

The effectiveness of the meeting will be severely compromised if any one of your invitees declines the invitation (assuming that you only invited those needed to achieve your purpose). Then, you must investigate whether or not they received (and understood) the publicity and had a sufficiently focused WIIFM.

If they fail to arrive at the appointed time (despite their earlier agreement to attend), there might be a multitude of reasons for their absence. You may need to be sensitive here – but it mustn't stop you investigating.

You have two choices in respect of someone not attending a meeting – is there a substitute with the necessary authority to contribute, commit and act? If not, adjourn the meeting until everyone necessary can attend.

Different roles within meetings

Roles and responsibilities are frequently combined – that's okay, providing nothing is missed. Each meeting requires an organizer, a chairperson, a timekeeper, a scribe/notetaker, at least one facilitator and participants.

The organizer

So what needs to be organized? Well, there are the logistics – the location, the equipment, any support materials, the timing, possibly transport. But let's not forget the participants – do they know they are supposed to attend, why they have been invited and what is required of them during the meeting?

And someone needs to check (before it's too late) that all of the above has taken place.

The chairperson

Some people prefer the name 'coordinator'. Fine – as long as the role is performed.

> **The line manager is not necessarily the best chairperson.**

While it might be true that the line manager can exercise control most easily, it can stilt others' contributions (they might wait to see what the chairperson thinks before commenting). Strictly speaking, the chairperson should be objective, independent and not express an opinion. Some line managers will find this very difficult!

> If the chairperson wants to express their opinions and thoughts, they should hand their role to someone else.

So what should the chairperson do?

- start the meeting on time. Agree and seek adherence to an appropriate style and the ground rules

- keep the meeting focused within the structure, agenda and time-scales

- ensure that everyone contributes (or why else have they been invited?) in a balanced way

- interpret the tone of voice and body language of participants (as well as listen to their views) and act accordingly

- in highly formal meetings, exercise a casting vote if necessary

- summarize each concluded item, consulting as to whether or not the purpose has been achieved and who, as a result, carries responsibility for what

- manage conflict (see Chapter 7) as appropriate

- summarize all outcomes before closing the meeting

- lead an evaluation of the effectiveness of the meeting

- close the meeting on schedule

- review the meeting notes prior to distribution.

However, too rigid an application of the role or

responsibilities can be destructive. Always remain flexible – be the leader of a meeting rather than its controller.

The timekeeper

The meeting should start and finish on time, with each part of the agenda staying within its allotted time (and that includes any breaks). It may be necessary to allot (and monitor) time limits for each person to express their views. Should any timed event be overturned or amended, it is the timekeeper's role to clarify the consequences of any change – although:

> **Too rigid an adherence to timekeeping can stilt the meeting's flow.**

It is likely, except in very large meetings, that this role is combined with another.

The scribe

One person should take notes – perhaps a personal assistant or secretary, maybe a participant (perhaps a different participant each time for a sequence of meetings).

> **It can be said that the most powerful person in a meeting is the scribe.**

This 'power' emanates from the fact that outcomes are recorded – and how they are recorded influences what will and will not be done as a result. For example: if a scribe disagrees with a decision, it is not unusual for the less-than-ethical scribe to note that further consideration is required!

The ethical scribe must:

- take notes in accordance with the pre-determined needs of participants. Do they need minutes or action points? (See Chapter 9)
- note each summary by the chairperson
- ask and/or challenge any uncertainty during the meeting in respect of that to be noted
- format the notes for review by the chairperson prior to distribution
- ensure the notes are distributed as soon as possible. The quickest way would be for the scribe to enter the notes on a networked computer during the meeting and, as the meeting ends, e-mail them to each attendee. The notes would probably arrive at their desks before they do! The downside to this practice is that the chairperson would not have any opportunity to review the content prior to distribution.

And, of course, accuracy is vital. In formal meetings, word-for-word accuracy is essential for the proposing, seconding and voting on resolutions/ motions, perhaps with an amending motion/rider (also requiring a proposer and seconder).

The facilitator

The role of facilitator is to make things easier than would otherwise be the case. It takes over much of the role and responsibilities of the chairperson – albeit with the utmost neutrality.

It can be introduced formally when the purpose is likely to be contentious or difficult to attain and/or there is a potential need for tools and techniques to overcome structural/style difficulties. In such cases, the role will typically be fulfilled by someone from a different part of the business than the participants – if not from an external specialist organization.

Informally:

> Every participant has a full obligation to fa-cilitate – to make 'easy' – the achievement of the meeting's purpose.

The participant

The simple answer to 'What should the participant do?' is:

> Do everything in this guide!

A more detailed answer would be:

- challenge the calling of any meeting which they believe to be unnecessary (from a general and personal perspective)

- understand why they have been invited to attend
- prepare thoroughly
- bring appropriate information, input and understanding to the meeting
- keep to the agreed timescales
- stay attentive, listening to all contributions
- contribute constructively and honestly
- be courteous and respectful to the subject and others
- perform whatever role is required of them
- ensure they receive the follow-up notes and challenge any which differ from their expectations or understanding
- fulfill any responsibility allotted during the meeting (and presumably specified in the notes)
- cascade information to others after the meeting (if appropriate)

> And if the meeting is, in some way, failing, act! An effective meeting is everyone's responsibility.

In summary

- think carefully about who to invite – and who not to. Who is required to achieve the meeting's purpose?

- it is better to invite disruptive influences because they may only seek to damage the meeting's outcomes later. Perhaps others will be needed to ensure a meeting remains balanced

- consider inviting people part-time if they only need to input on specific agenda items

- pay attention to effective advance publicity for a meeting, ensuring, amongst other things, that enough time is given for individuals to prepare

- don't assume people will automatically accept an invitation to a meeting, or prepare thoroughly or contribute effectively – they must be motivated by the organizer and chairperson

- if would-be participants cannot or do not attend, it is highly likely that the meeting should be rescheduled since the achievement of the purpose would be in doubt

- meetings should be led rather than controlled

- roles and responsibilities in meetings are frequently combined

- every meeting should be organized, chaired, kept to time and noted

- a formal facilitator role may be desirable for contentious issues or when everyone there wishes to express an opinion

- participants all have responsibility in a meeting –

if any specific role is not being performed effectively, each has the responsibility to help and support each other to deliver the intended outcomes

- too rigid an application of any role or responsibility can be destructive

- all meeting participants should keep to the agreed
timescales, stay attentive, contribute constructively
and honestly with courtesy and respect.

_____

4
The agenda

When the purpose, style and number of participants has been determined, an agenda can be developed. An agenda has:

- the date and start/finish times of the meeting
- a distribution list itemizing who is to attend and an allocation of the meeting's standard roles (chairperson, scribe etc)
- the location of the meeting (see next chapter)
- whether or not refreshments will be provided
- the purpose(s) of the meeting.

And against each purpose, specify …

- a timescale
- any special contributions (for instance, *'This discussion will be led by John, who will start with a 15-minute presentation of the key facts'*)

- a reference to (if not supply of) any supporting documentation. There is little point in distributing masses of information during a meeting – far better to distribute it for reading in advance and spend the time in the meeting discussing rather than reading
- a statement as to any specific preparation that is required
- anyone who will be joining the meeting for a specific item.

Hidden or personal agendas

It seems appropriate here to mention 'hidden agendas', where a meeting purports to have one purpose and in reality is for something quite different. This might be the intent of those calling the meeting, or when a participant seeks to use any opportunity to pursue a personal agenda (which may or may not have anything to do with the purpose).

If you suspect that there is a hidden agenda, adjourn and seek one-to-one clarification with the initiator of it.

However, be aware that there may not be a hidden agenda – it could simply be a misinterpretation of events.

Start times

An agenda needs to state when the meeting will start!
Think about:

- when would be convenient for participants? (Perhaps they have to 'cover' their colleagues' telephones over lunch etc?)

- how long will it take each person to travel to and from the meeting?

- is there a danger that people might get distracted with other issues at certain times of the day. For example: if a meeting is scheduled to start half an hour after everyone arrives at work, might they get into other work (or simply waste that time) before it starts?

- how long will it take to set up the meeting room?

- what times of day are participants most likely to be alert?

> **Don't assume that meetings have to start on the hour or half hour.**

Setting a meeting at an unusual time can help people to arrive on time (strange though it is). So how about starting at ten minutes past eleven to see what happens?

If there is one 'golden rule' about start times, it is:

> **Always start a meeting at the stated time.**

It is discourteous to those who arrive on time, to expect them to sit and wait for those who are late or talking on the telephone. If your meetings always start late, you are encouraging everyone not to bother being punctual – so as a result, future meetings start later and later.

Structuring a meeting

All meetings should have a structure with a beginning, middle and end.

And the structure will be summarized in the agenda. Let's look at the components of an effective structure in more detail:

The beginning of a meeting

There is much to do to open an effective meeting:

- welcome those present and thank them for giving their time to attend

- check that everyone has received the agenda in advance and has a copy with them (have some spares ready)

- emphasize the purpose(s) of the meeting and check for broad understanding

- introduce anyone who is new to the rest of group (perhaps give out name cards). If the group has come together for the first time, a brief introduction of everyone may be appropriate, as if they introduce themselves, this could take considerable time

- explain everyone's role within the meeting

- present any apologies for absence (this tends to be used when the style of meeting is relatively formal). Remember that an individual's absence could prevent achievement of the meeting's purpose and it might need to be adjourned

- verify that any required 'quorum' is met. (Some meetings cannot constitutionally be held unless a certain number of people are present)

- describe the 'domestic arrangements'. These would depend on the existing knowledge of each person but it could include: the emergency evacuation procedure, health and safety issues, toilet/washroom locations, provision of refreshments, how messages from outside of the meeting should be handled and a request to turn off mobile phones and pagers – unless essential

- explain how any record of the meeting will be kept and to what level of detail

- state the finish time of the meeting

- check for any questions

- if appropriate, update the meeting on issues from any prior meeting, (such as the progress achieved, whether or not anything has changed and any inhibitors to success). If this is likely to take considerable time, it should be a separate agenda item

- recommend how any issues which arise during the meeting that are not on the agenda will be managed. Typically, this will be a note-taking process to structure future agendas.

The middle of a meeting

> The greatest priorities should be at the top of the agenda.

However:

> It is better to schedule contentious items before a break, which will allow a 'cooling-off' period.

Breaks are always useful during meetings even if there are not contentious items – it allows people to recharge as well as take a comfort stop or get a drink.

If an agenda item is not achieved within the allotted timeframe, the meeting has a decision to make: to defer it to another meeting or to extend the timeframe? If the latter, the consequences of giving it more time have to be clearly identified, understood and agreed by all.

As each agenda item is completed, the chairperson must:

> Summarize the outcome, ensure everyone agrees with it and the responsibility for any follow up is clearly identified.

The end of a meeting

Well this should be easy! Perhaps 'let's get out of here!'

Sorry – not so fast. Whenever I am training, as the session draws to its close there is a tendency for people to start looking at their watches, tidy up their papers (if not put them away) and even put on their coats! We haven't finished – there's more – so:

> **As the end approaches, tell everyone what is left to do!**

At the end of the meeting:

- summarize the outcome of each agenda item. This would include checking that everyone clearly understands what they have committed to do over fixed timescales

- state any outstanding issues and how they are to be dealt with in the future

- validate that the purpose(s) of the meeting has (have) been met – and if not, identify the cause and how it will be resolved

- check for outstanding questions

- evaluate whether or not the meeting met the expectations of the participants. If the meeting were to start again, would they like it to be different in some way?

- review whether or not the meeting has delivered the targeted added value?

- set (if required) the date and general location for

the next meeting

- thank attendees for their input, recognizing any success achieved through the meeting

- close the meeting.

'Any other business' (AOB)

A good agenda will have been constructed through consultation with the participants. Any proposed additions to an agenda during a meeting should be actively discouraged (since no one has had the opportunity to prepare) – and that extends to AOB – which is why it does not appear in the above section on closing the meeting.

My antipathy to AOB is, in part, due to the abuse of the meetings process it often symbolizes. I have worked alongside someone who sought to use AOB for contentious statements, knowing that there was little time for discussion. Since the participants had already started to mentally withdraw from the meeting, he tried for a quick agreement to allow everyone to leave the meeting. It worked initially – until we realized what he was doing.

On a more objective note, AOB is a set of surprises for participants. As such, they have had no time to prepare for anything discussed under this heading – therefore, there is no point in introducing them. I can hear a note of protest:

> **What if something urgent occurs after the agenda has been distributed?**
> **Simple: call a separate meeting to discuss it.**

And:

> If it is too minor a point for the agenda,
> it is too minor a point for a meeting.

In summary, AOB is a poor excuse for a bad and incomplete agenda. But before banning AOB, let participants know in advance that it is being replaced with a more complete agenda.

Finish time

Having defined the agenda, add each item's timeframe together (and not forgetting time for the opening and close of the meeting): the finish time will be self-evident.

> If 10 minutes is sufficient to achieve the meeting's purpose, schedule only 10 minutes.

Never overrun the finish time – it is disrespectful to participants to assume that whatever they had planned to do after the meeting is less important. Secure participants' gratitude by seeking to fulfill the purpose and end the meeting early!

If your meetings traditionally run late:

> Schedule a meeting to finish either at participants' lunch time or when they would normally finish for the day.

Such meetings usually do finish on time – assuming you aren't providing a free lunch!

In summary

- every meeting should have an agenda distributed in advance, clearly stating the meeting's purpose with supporting details

- perceived hidden agendas should be challenged during an adjournment

- determine the best time to start a meeting and then stick to it

- meetings should have a structure that is commensurate with the declared purpose(s) – although all structures have a beginning, middle and end

- summarize each agenda item as it is completed and say what is going to happen as a result

- the finish time can only be determined after the agenda has been formulated

- finishing early is always well received!

- the use of 'any other business' often represents an abuse of the principles of effective meetings

- important new issues should be the subject of a separate meeting – track any issues arising during a meeting for later consideration

- don't skimp on an effective close to a meeting and do include an assessment of the degree of success achieved as a result of coming together.

5
The location

The general location

Too often, the chairperson or organizer will have participants come to them, however inconvenient (or costly) it is for everyone else. It's called 'the exercise of power' and is not to be condoned.

> The chosen location should balance everyone's needs, convenience and costs.

Rarely, however, will such a balance be easy. Think about where the majority will be travelling from, the needs of part-time attendees and the difficulties that any individual might have in reaching a location – especially if they have no private transport.

The specific location

Having established the general location, we can consider the meeting venue itself. A number of factors should be considered here – first:

> Think about the type and style of venue that would most suit the purpose of the meeting.

For example: Would it be appropriate to tell someone they are redundant in an expensive restaurant? I don't think so!

The venue should be accessible to all (including those with disabilities) and provide the necessary elements for success: minimal disruption/distraction, appropriate atmosphere, required equipment, the right size of room (for the numbers invited) and the right infrastructure (car parking, refreshments, food and perhaps overnight accommodation). And all of these should not only be readily available but also of a requisite standard.

The cheaper option will frequently be to stay 'on-site' rather than, for instance, book a room in a hotel or conference centre. But consider the implications of working on-site where interruptions are likely and people are checking their desk or e-mails at every break.

Eat and meet

'Let's have a breakfast meeting – or lunch.' Fine, although indigestion may be on the menu! Consider:

- who's going to pay? the person extending the invite or the person who gets the most from it?

- dining tables rarely have space for papers or to make notes

- privacy cannot (usually) be guaranteed

- alcohol (even one glass of wine over dinner) can have an effect on what is said and done – are you prepared to run the risk?

- some people have poor eating habits! Prepare to be put off!

Food and drink

A thirsty or hungry person cannot stay attentive – their concentration will lapse and participation diminish. So some food or drink may be appropriate in a meeting room as it is more likely to keep them attentive. I say 'more likely' because a heavy meal is, as most of us are aware, quite likely to send some people to sleep!

Drinks (the non-alcoholic kind) can avoid the need to break the meeting, but then a protracted meeting (anything over say one and a half hours) should always give participants a break – if only to go to the toilet/washroom or get some fresh air. Fresh air is great if participants are looking tired or the atmosphere in the meeting is getting somewhat overheated.

On the negative side, providing food or drink can be difficult to 'get right'. How do they like their coffee? Do they want their water sparkling or still? Chilled or iced? There is also the possibility that the meeting will naturally extend until lunch is served when it could have finished hours ago. And of course, there's the potential mess or spillage – to reduce the likelihood of this, always break the meeting while people eat.

Whatever your decision on food and drink, advise participants in advance what will, and what will not, be provided – going to a breakfast meeting only to find we don't eat breakfast can be very annoying!

Layout of the room

So what layout would suit the meeting's purpose? Let's look at the options:

- **a circle**: be it of chairs or chairs and tables. This encourages the feeling that all participants (and therefore their views) carry equal weight. It can, however, be harder for the chairperson to exercise control (should it be necessary). Tables are often seen as a 'barrier' to openness, but they might be necessary for people to make or refer to notes

- **a 'C' or 'U' shaped layout** where a circle of chairs and/or tables is 'broken' on one side to allow the chairperson or facilitator to use that space. Frequently used by trainers as their preferred layout, it allows some exercise of control simply because the visual focus will always be towards the broken side, albeit everyone should be able to establish eye contact with everyone else

- **a boardroom layout**: here the chairperson can exercise control from the 'head' of the table – the only person who can be seen clearly by everyone. This can stilt the potential contribution of some participants. Some may seek out the more 'powerful' seats around the table to exert influence (see influential seating, page 54)

- **standing**: ban people from leaning or sitting on anything! This can be very hard going on people with back trouble, but:

> Stand-only meetings tend to be short meetings!

The above layouts are unlikely to work with large groups when others could be considered:

- **'theatre' style** – but discussion between participants is difficult due to the lack of eye contact
- **the amphitheatre**: the chairperson/speaker sits or stands in the centre point and is surrounded by participants. Everyone has good eye contact and it projects a sense of 'nothing-to-fear' by the speaker. (Thus favoured by some politicians)

In reality, there are no suitable layouts for large meetings – but then:

> There are few meetings that will achieve their purpose if there are too many people there.

So accept large groups for what such a gathering will become – a one-sided presentation with perhaps a few questions.

Influential seating

Fairly obviously, many layouts favour the chairperson in terms of visibility and control. But there are certain other seats that offer a sense of 'power' to participants.

The first people into a meeting room can reveal a lot about their attitude – their play for power – by where they choose to sit. (Naturally, later arrivals have a limited choice and therefore are not so revealing).

Power seating includes:

- the seat at the **opposite end** of a boardroom table to the chairperson. This person might be challenging the authority of the chair

- the seat immediately **next to** the chairperson is generally viewed as supportive of the chair but also 'sharing' their authority (if not basking in it). The seat at the chairperson's right hand is more indicative of this

- a person who deliberately sits **opposite someone already seated** might indicate that they expect to be of opposing views

- **sitting in cliques**: this can make people bolder in expressing views, encourage whispering and the passing of notes which can undermine the chairperson and other contributors.

However:

> Influential seating can be used positively to serve the meeting's purpose.

For instance: if you know someone is going to oppose your opinions during a meeting, the most 'powerful' chair is the one next to them. People find it difficult to argue with someone when sitting immediately next to them.

One alternative is to put name cards at each place before anyone arrives to counterbalance anticipated power plays.

Supplies and equipment

Pens, paper, laptop? Think it through during your preparation and ensure that everything that might be required will be available when you need it.

If equipment has to be adjusted/set up midway through a meeting, think about declaring a 'comfort stop' for everyone while it is undertaken.

Electronic meetings

You may recall from Chapter 1 that a meeting is 'a gathering of more than one person for a specific purpose' – although not necessarily in the same room. Thus, we can have 'electronic meetings', where participants in different locations watch, listen and speak 'live' to each other via technology.

Participants in different rooms (perhaps in different countries) are on camera and the images are projected in all of the locations. You can therefore also see yourself. Each room has microphones, so everyone can hear each other. Other technology may be used which allows everyone to share the images from whatever visual aids are used in any location.

This is an enormous subject – its popularity and availability is growing by the day and the technology is advancing all the time. It is only discussed briefly *as a specific issue* in this guide, but here are some key pointers:

> **Almost all of the tools, techniques and advice in this guide are readily transferable for use in electronic meetings.**

However, there are some extra challenges:

- it can be difficult to non-verbally 'signal' that you want everyone's attention

- it is difficult to maintain eye contact on camera – yet it is sometimes essential to show determination and confidence with a specific individual. So use people's names often

- it does not – yet – provide stimulus to all the human senses: For example. I am not aware of any technology that can stimulate 'smell'

- people watching a screen can become incredibly aware of others' (bad) habits and suspicious of others' sincerity far quicker than in real life

- the camera and microphone can pick up some content that it would have been better to miss – the negative 'rolling' of the eyes, any 'whispering' etc.

- participants can find this quite intense, so frequent breaks are advisable

- the effectiveness of the meeting will hinge on the technology. If it fails, the meeting can't proceed.

So make sure every location has someone who understands the technology!

On the positive side, electronic meetings can bring people together at very short notice and minimize travel costs – especially for an international gathering, but remember:

- take account of time-zones – a time acceptable to you, may be the middle of the night for others
- cultural differences should be accommodated.

In summary

- choose a general location which balances everyone's needs, convenience and costs
- the choice of location – right down to the room and its layout – should support the meeting's purpose (and therefore its style and structure)
- meeting at the place of someone's work may appear cheaper – but only if they can fully concentrate on the meeting itself
- eating during a meeting has many negatives – but not providing drink or food when participants need them will disrupt their concentration
- some seating arrangements have 'power' (or influential) seats, use this positively to support your meeting's purpose
- always ensure that all the possible needs in respect of supplies and equipment are anticipated in

advance and then provided

- electronic meetings are an increasingly popular means of communicating, but have extra challenges attached to them.

6
Let's do it!

It's Chapter 6 and we are finally ready to start our meeting. And there's one basic rule:

> **Secure the right participation!**

So everyone starts to arrive in a timely manner, agenda in hand. You have already organized the room – if not the seating plan – and you want to get everything off to a flying start. So what now?

First impressions count! Be ready and welcome people as they arrive. Perhaps informally introduce them to each other (if they haven't met before). Make sure they know where the toilets/washrooms are and how they can get themselves something to drink.

Call the meeting 'to order' and start on time.

Ground rules

As part of the opening, it can be useful to establish 'ground rules' – especially if there is a possibility of a contentious issue or a need for confidentiality …

So what sort of 'rules' might there be? Well, it's not rocket science – more common sense. Perhaps confidentiality, freedom of speech, integrity and honesty – with no blame!, mutual respect, listen to each other, no interrupting, retain focus, maintain momentum, stick to all timescales (including breaks) and possibly follow a pre-determined process – for instance, on how a group decision will be made.

> **Ground rules are most likely to be adhered to if developed by all participants rather than presented to them.**

And:

> **If ground rules are 'breached' during the meeting, the onus is on everyone to act.**

If meetings have pre-established ground rules, it is still appropriate to re-visit them regularly.

'Ice-breakers'

These can help a meeting get underway quickly and are particularly useful if people are meeting for the first time. Their purpose is to get people talking and relaxed – but not too talkative nor too relaxed! Here are a few ideas:

- ask people to introduce themselves in an unusual way – perhaps by drawing a picture of themselves in and outside of work. Keep this simple and basic – you don't want to intimidate people before you get started!

- ask people to talk with the person on their right and then to introduce that person to the group

- allow participants to wander around the room finding something they have in common with at least two other people – and share their conclusions with the rest of the group. It might be that John lives at number 13 – and so does Jenny (but different roads!). And John holidayed in France last year – and so did Gerry

- a quick 'game' can break the ice – perhaps charades (miming the name of a book, film or whatever). Be careful – you don't want any winners or losers and some participants might consider 'fun' ice-breakers a waste of time and/or patronizing.

There are many options here – but not all will work for a particular meeting:

> The purpose, structure and style of a meeting – as well as participants' own cultures – will dictate the appropriateness of an ice-breaker.

Keeping people on track

One sure way to get off the subject is to abandon the agenda – but assuming that does not happen, why might a meeting de-rail? Well a simple lack of control (by the chairperson), lost concentration or simply boredom! A meeting can also be deliberately taken off track if someone feels 'cornered'.

For instance, a former colleague used to interrupt a discussion with a joke. The first few times it happened, I was totally baffled – then I realized that he did it whenever his opinion was on the verge of being overturned.

So what can be done to keep on track?

1   Restate the meeting's purpose and timeframe

2   Remind everyone of any agreed ground rules

3   Consider a five-minute break (and start afresh upon everyone's return)

4   Stress that a rejection of someone's view is not a rejection of that person, nor their contribution

5   Build on a spurious comment to bring things back to the agenda. Perhaps 'That's a good idea – what can we learn from that to help us with the issue in hand?'

6   Close off a discussion by stating that it should be noted for consideration at a later time.

And remember:

Everyone has a responsibility to pull a meeting back onto the agenda. However, accept that occasional tangents are acceptable (if brief).

The attention span of a gnat

To be honest, I have no idea what the attention span of a gnat is! However, the message here is that people's attention will 'wander' if they are:

- unsure why they are there
- feeling that their opinions are being ignored or disrespected
- believe they are wasting their time (for instance, that a decision has already been made irrespective of what they say)
- under significant pressure/stress to be doing other things – a belief which might be totally self-imposed
- tired, in need of refreshment or a comfort break.

Yet again, the answers are as stated many times in this guide: don't call a meeting unless it has a specific purpose, motivate each individual to participate, produce an agenda and stick to it, control the meeting's progress, work within agreed timeframes and emphasize the anticipated added value from a successful outcome to the meeting.

It also means that *if* the meeting has to be relatively long, provide 'time-outs' and ample opportunity for people to talk/participate in some way, which that will keep them far more alert than simply listening to others.

A lack of participation

Perhaps you would rather that we discuss how to discourage participation by those talking too much! Well, we will in Chapter 7. But for now, let's look at a lack of participation by the 'quieter' ones.

> **Remember – since you only invite those needed to achieve the purpose of the meeting, everyone must contribute.**

There could be lots of reasons why people fail to participate – maybe they are intimidated by others in the meeting (for instance, their line manager), await others' views or think their own views might be considered naïve, stupid or disruptive. Perhaps they feel they never have the chance to speak because others never stop talking – or they may just prefer to listen and reflect further before saying anything. Whatever the reason:

> **It is the prime responsibility of the chairperson to ensure everyone contributes, but no one is exempt from this responsibility.**

Encouraging participation

Before the meeting starts, check that everyone knows

why they have been invited, the role they have in the meeting and that they are motivated to attend and participate. Reiterate the purpose of the meeting and the anticipated added value from a successful outcome.

Then, review the participants' relationships. Do you need to talk with individuals in advance to ensure their comfort level? Consider asking line managers to hold back on their opinions until others have spoken or whether or not staff and line managers should attend different meetings.

At the start of the meeting, once again, reiterate the purpose of the meeting, emphasizing the value to be placed on each attendee's contribution.

To increase an individual's participation during the meeting:

- state their name upfront and ask them a broad question about the subject. (If you start with a complicated or specific question, it could deter them further). Follow this through with a more detailed question

- look (but don't stare) directly at the individual

- if someone else interrupts, signal them to stop

- support/praise early contributions from the quiet ones – yes, even if you don't agree!

- at break-time, check on a one-to-one whether or not the meeting is fulfilling the needs/expectations of anyone who has remained quiet, and encourage their future participation.

Note that this section should be read in tandem with the later section on too much participation:

> Securing participation from one is also about controlling the over-contribution of another.

Asking questions

The right questions will facilitate success in a meeting:

- **ease people gradually** into discussing difficult issues don't 'go for the jugular' as an opener – they will act defensively

- **ask 'open' questions** to solicit a range of possible answers and open up a discussion … Typically, these start with: How? Why? When? What? Who? or Where?

- **give participants time to adjust** between listening and then talking (perhaps after a presentation)

- **if you don't understand, ask!** 'Can you clarify that for me – I'm not sure I understand?' or 'Have I understood correctly – are you saying …?'

- **use questioning** if the discussion is losing its focus or momentum: 'Let's see where we have got to – I believe we are saying … is that right?'

However:

> The wrong questions will distort the outcome of a meeting – be it from the chairperson or a participant.

For instance: 'Would you all agree with me that ...?' or 'Is it not true to say that ...?' These are leading questions – they reveal the answer that the questioner seeks and thus suppress others' opinions.

Answering questions

Answer succinctly!

> The longer the answer, the more likely it will be viewed as weak, spurious or evasive.

If your answer *has* to be long, restate the question at intervals to show you are still focused. One way to do this and avoid interruptions is to say:

'There are four key points here. First ..., second ...' etc. It is unlikely that you will get interrupted until you reach your last point because everyone knows you have more to say – all the more so if you give the most important information early in your answer.

If you don't know the answer, be honest but commit to finding out.

In summary

- be ready before the attendees start arriving
- consider asking attendees to define the ground rules for a successful meeting
- consider 'ice-breakers' to help everyone to get to

know each other and feel comfortable – providing it fits with the purpose, structure and style of a meeting and the participants' culture

- since those invited are needed to achieve the objective of the meeting, everyone must participate
- everyone is responsible for ensuring everyone stays on track
- work to ensure that everyone's attention is maintained
- secure valuable contributions by acting both before and during the meeting
- asking the right questions encourages success; the wrong questions will destroy the value of this and future meetings
- check for understanding and summarize at regular points during a meeting
- answer questions succinctly.

7
Get your point across – quickly

An effective message can and should be put across in less than 100 words.

For example:

You have spent money to buy this guide. A very sensible – a wise – move on your behalf because who wants to waste their time in boring, ineffective meetings? Was it worth the money? If you save just a couple of hours, your company will believe so – and so will you if you are a little less stressed or a little earlier home one evening. So read on – there's lots of hours to be saved by this – and all the other guides – in the series!

I make that 86 words. And my message is all there.

So what has been done here? Well, I got your attention (by talking about you spending your money!) and a bit of flattery (being sensible and wise in your purchase). I then gave you the 'What's in it for me?' (saving time, reducing stress, getting home a little earlier) and ended on a positive note (read on for more!).

So when you need to get your point across, gain their attention; set the scene (that is, explain briefly what you are talking about); give them the benefits of your proposal and ensure that the overall theme is constructive and positive. Anticipate potential objections and provide a counterbalance within your 100 words.

Deliver your message confidently, maintaining eye contact, a strong/clear tone of voice and positive body language.

However, it is worth bearing in mind that:

> The first and last ideas in a discussion are rarely accepted. The ideas which are advocated or developed during it typically gain most support.

And on a cautionary note:

> Just because you can influence others, it does not mean you always have the best ideas!

Getting difficult messages through – in advance

If you know that some agenda items are going to be difficult then identify influential attendees in advance and 'lobby' for their support and/or an appropriate level of involvement. In other words, you can lobby someone to speak up – but you can also lobby someone to keep quiet!

There are positive and negative aspects to lobbying. It can create balance in a meeting that would otherwise be a one-sided discussion. And by dealing with an individual's concerns in advance, it can help keep the agenda on time.

However

> Lobbying infers that the outcome is already determined.

If so, why is there a meeting at all?

Getting difficult messages through – during a meeting

There are a number of techniques available here:

- use a facilitator to balance the discussion and allow the chairperson to express their own point of view

- if this is a 'fait-accompli' – for example, a decision has already been made and is being presented to the meeting – consider how participants may have some input. People are far more accepting of change if they have some meaningful involvement

- ask for a brief comment from each participant. Start by asking someone with positive views – but not too obviously! Do not allow any one person to take over.

- don't allow broad generalizations of disagreement. If people disagree, ask them to specify exactly what part of the issue they find contentious. Ask for evidence – opinions and thoughts must be substantiated

As the chairperson of many meetings, one lady (who went on to become Deputy MD of a major UK retailer) asked me how I always managed to get contentious issues through my meetings with such apparent ease.

Simply, I placed a difficult issue immediately after an issue in the agenda on which I had no real opinion. On introducing the first, I would see what the opinion of the meeting was and then oppose that view – eventually conceding the point to the meeting. For the next (and contentious) issue, I would lead the discussion with my perspective and, in the spirit of fairness, the group concluded that since they had won the last point, I should win the next – and so I did.

I would like to think my approach remained ethical and fair throughout. Certainly the lady in question thought so – but you may judge me on that for yourselves. (Perhaps as Chairman I should have had less to say?) Therefore:

> Don't fight every point. Choose when you want to be most influential.

Getting difficult messages through – afterwards?

Forget it – you're too late. If you issue a difficult message after a meeting, people will be suspicious of your motives and challenge you in the future. If you try to reverse a decision after a meeting has closed, you would destroy the purpose of that meeting – and cloud all future meetings with suspicion. However, you might be able to challenge a decision after a meeting if genuinely new and relevant information comes to light.

Conflict and meetings

Conflict will occur in meetings. In fact, it is unlikely that successful decisions can be reached without conflict (better described as disagreement). The opposite extreme is that everyone says 'yes' to the very first suggestion – and that is suspicious.

While some conflict is appropriate and healthy, there are some types of conflict which are not acceptable – such as personal attacks:

> **Inappropriate conflict must be dealt with.**

Let's look at conflict in more detail.

Causes of conflict

There are five possible causes of conflict:

1 Where people are expected to do something which they believe to be unreasonable

2 Where people are in conflict with the 'society' (or group) with which they interact

3 Where there are opposing needs, wants and opinions

4 Where people have unreasonable expectations of themselves

5 Where people have to act against their own belief systems/code.

The first three causes are what we might refer to as external conflict – the last two are internal (that is, conflict within oneself). However, even if the cause is internal, it can still manifest itself against others. For example:

Being asked to do something in a meeting which is against your principles/ethics (such as dismissing someone whose 'face does not fit') might manifest itself in an argument on its validity rather than because you feel uncomfortable about doing it.

So what should be done if there is conflict – permit or control it? The answer depends upon two factors: the cause of the conflict and how it manifests itself. Let's look again at the five causes and how we should react:

1 **Where people are expected to do something unreasonable**. The person being asked is the judge of what is and is not 'reasonable' here. This problem usually arises because either those asked misunderstand what the expectation actually is or those asking fail to appreciate the impact of their request. For example:

A meeting could erupt in conflict when a manager requires the participants to identify savings in staff costs. Participants might fear redundancy or dismissal – yet the manager may be looking for savings against future recruitment. Or the manager may be failing to appreciate the negative effect on the business of not recruiting more staff. If such conflict occurs, encourage an honest and accurate exchange of opinions, thoughts and feelings *after the facts have been clarified*

2   **Conflict with society**. If someone makes a sexist remark, they will be (I trust) in conflict with their organization's culture. The chairperson should address it immediately and forcibly, giving an explanation (but not a justification) of why it is inappropriate. Conflict with a society has three possible outcomes – adherence, removal (from the meeting) or face the consequences (potential disciplinary action)

3   **Opposing needs, wants and opinions**. In a negotiation one party might want the cheapest possible deal – the other the highest possible price. So conflict is inevitable yet if stopped, the negotiation ends. Try to prevent people taking a specific position – one's ego can make it very difficult to change the expressed viewpoint. For example:

In a pay negotiation, one party seeks a 10% increase and the other only offers 3%. There is conflict – but to avoid escalating conflict, discuss what has made the parties adopt those percentages (rather than the percentages themselves). Perhaps both sides seek the industry standard, but have different views on what that is. Establishing the facts about the industrial standard provides a way forward away from conflict

4 **Unreasonable expectations of oneself**. Maybe someone tries to do things beyond their capability. They might, for instance, take on too great a commitment in a meeting and have, in doing so, set themselves up to fail. Such people should be guided and supported not to place too high an expectation upon themselves

5 **Acting against one's own beliefs**. This can be difficult to recognize, although the more surprising a reluctance to act is, the more likely it is that this is the cause. For instance:

An unusual refusal to work overtime might disguise a person protecting their family values or religious beliefs. This individual needs to be encouraged to feel comfortable about expressing such without fear of ridicule, repression or discrimination, which would probably be easier handled on a one-to-one basis.

> In general, most causes of conflict can be worked through in a meeting.

Manifested conflict

There are different ways that people can behave when in conflict:

- with a **reasonable** tone and expression

- by **shouting** and/or **aggressive** body language

- by **crying** (actual, pretence or on the verge of), being upset, conceding key points

- by making **snide or sceptical** comments

- by **withdrawing** from making any contribution, being uncooperative, stalling, introducing diversionary tactics

- by making **personal attacks** be it verbal insults or physical threats and violence. (Take *immediate* action in respect of such attacks).

Fairly obviously, the first is fine – in fact, it is healthy because the outcome will have been tested rather than just acquiesced. The latter are not acceptable. So what should be done when inappropriate conflict is manifested?

First, stay calm! Re-affirm any ground rules and request everyone to work within them. (Perhaps further rules need to be added – although it is probably too late for this meeting). Whatever your role in the meeting, don't take sides but do 'protect' anyone being personally attacked. Move the discussion onto facts and common ground only – avoid opinions or thoughts until a more constructive atmosphere pervades.

If that fails, adjourn the meeting and speak with both parties in the conflict on a one-to-one basis. Identify the cause of the conflict and gain agreement on an acceptable way forward. Apologies may be appropriate – in extreme cases, perhaps when the meeting re-starts.

Upon reconvening, restate the purpose of the meeting and the ground rules. Then summarize the *progress* to date (any agreements between the parties and/or common ground). Do not re-introduce what caused the conflict directly but take a different approach. For example, rather than accuse someone of failing to deliver, discuss what needs to happen to enhance delivery in the future.

Take greater control of the meeting until the contentious area is dealt with and then revert to the earlier style.

If the behaviour reoccurs, set a new meeting date and close the meeting – and don't be swayed by people 'promising not to do it again'. If a new meeting is scheduled, devise a new approach to avoid the same pitfall.

To summarize:

> Conflict has a role to play in an effective meeting.
> However, inappropriate behaviour does not.

Anticipating conflict

> Determining the right response to conflict is much easier if it is anticipated.

So when the purpose and agenda is published, consider the potential reactions and interests of each participant. If you are uncertain as to how anyone might react, find out!

Should you anticipate the potential for conflict – and some is healthy – consider lobbying for support and counterbalance. Seek an agreement on some ground rules at the start of the meeting. Then think how the discussion can best be managed.

And remember the expression:

> **No pain, no gain**

In summary

- prepare what you want to say in less than 100 words – but don't fight every battle
- being good at influencing doesn't make you right
- lobby in advance to create a balanced viewpoint but don't make the meeting become a 'rubber-stamp' to support your views
- consider whether or not the agenda sequence should be adjusted to ease progress
- don't try to challenge the outcome of a meeting after the event unless there is new information
- conflict is healthy to improve a meeting's outcome – but not if it includes personal attacks and/or negative behaviours
- inappropriate conflict must be dealt with and knowing the cause can facilitate a response
- clarification and understanding – especially of the facts – will negate much potential conflict
- avoid anyone in a conflict becoming entrenched
- understand, guide and support people who are demanding of themselves
- in times of conflict, use the ground rules

- adjournments can help people to 'cool-off'
- seek to identify potential conflict before the meeting starts and react accordingly
- consider discussing known/anticipated conflict outside of the meeting.

8
Building a consensus

A consensus is an outcome that everyone can 'go along with'.

It may not be everyone's first choice – it may not be anyone's first choice – but it is an outcome that everyone at the meeting is committed to support. And as such, it is frequently the goal that a meeting must seek. A meeting occurs to get everyone's opinion, so be surprised (and suspicious) if everyone offers immediate 100% support to an outcome!

So when a consensus is believed to have been achieved, ensure everyone is very clear about what they need to say and do when leaving the meeting. This should avoid the potential backstabbing or backtracking which might otherwise take place.

Depending upon the purpose of a meeting, it may be appropriate to use problem-solving and/or decision-making techniques to achieve a consensus.

Thinking creatively

Part of any problem-solving or decision-making process requires some element of creative thinking. And this will have an impact on the style and structure of a meeting:

> Creative thinking should be free-flowing and non-judgmental.

Problem solving in meetings

Good preparation for a meeting means that people will have considered a problem beforehand. But poor preparation can include making their mind up about a problem before the meeting begins. This is a difficult balance – so to start any problem solving session, emphasize that there needs to be a step-by-step approach to its resolution and whilst a note should be taken of any possible cause or solution, it should not be considered until all the facts are established.

There is also a tendency to address the effect of a problem rather than the cause. For instance, I might take a pain-killer for my headache. The headache goes away – problem solved? No – the effect is removed, but the reason (or cause) of my headache has not been addressed. And unless I address the cause, I will probably get another headache. Therefore:

> It is essential to adopt a structured approach to solving a problem in a meeting.

There are many problem-solving tools that could be adopted – but the principles are:

1 **Describe factually what the problem is**. The key word here is 'factually'. To say 'Our sales are down' is unhelpful. We need to know why our sales are down, by how much etc.

2 **Think creatively about all the possible causes of the problem**. Perhaps our product is no longer as fashionable as it once was or there are nation-wide distribution problems affecting every supplier? Maybe bad publicity has caused a market downturn.

3 **Through discussion, eliminate any potential causes which don't fit the facts**. For example, perhaps there has been no adverse publicity about our products which could have affected the sales.

4 **Select the 'most likely' cause from the remaining ideas**. We might determine that our sales are most likely being affected by a change in fashion.

5 **Ideally, test the most probable cause.** So for our falling sales – how might we test our theory that the product is no longer fashionable? Well, we could conduct a survey, or we could ask the fashion experts.

6 **Put a permanent solution in place to address the problem**. In our example, we might seek to

adapt the product to become fashionable again.

There will be, however, occasions when the effects of a problem should be addressed:

> If the problem cannot be resolved, minimizing the effects might be the only option.

Perhaps our product cannot be made more fashionable – so perhaps dropping our budget and cutting back production is the only way to avoid surplus stock. But if we do this every time fashion changes, we may have no business left – so think about the consequences of addressing only the effects, before taking such action.

'People problem solving'

People are not a 'problem' but their attitude, behaviour or performance may be an issue. So here we should examine the issue rather than the person. Providing you stick with this, the technique advocated will work well if:

> Those being analysed are part of the discussion since they are part of the solution.

(For more on managing people's performance, read the 'Easy Step By Step Guide, *Motivating Your Staff For Better Performance*)

Decision-making in meetings

A workable process for meetings is:

1 **Identify what the decision is** that is about to be made. So, we might meet to decide who will supply a new computer system.

2 **Describe factually** what the outcome of the decision must comply with. To put it simply, perhaps our computer system must be networked for up to 100 terminals, have specified licensed software for functionality and have a reliability rating averaging 98.7%. It must be installed within eight months and not exceed the allocated budget.

3 **Think creatively** about all possible decisions. In our example, we might select four possible suppliers.

4 Through discussion, **eliminate any potential decisions** which don't fit the prescribed outcome. Perhaps one supplier can't deliver on time and another is too expensive.

5 **Consider the positive and negative implications** from each possible decision. Of our two remaining potential suppliers, we could list the 'pros and cons' of each.

6 **Select the 'best' decision** from the remaining ideas. So on balance, which supplier would we prefer to choose?

7 Ideally**, test the 'best' decision** in some way to check you are about to make the right decision. We could, for instance, ask our chosen supplier to set up a mini-network for our staff to test.

8   Implement the decision – buy the network!

Make it visual

Whether creatively thinking, problem solving or decision making, it will help participants if:

> All information is recorded as the discussion progresses. For example: on a flip chart

In summary

- the consensus of a meeting does not imply that everyone is in total agreement – merely that they will abide by the decision.
- be suspicious if everyone agrees to an agenda issue
- creative thinking should be free-flowing and non-judgmental
- adopt a structure for solving problems and making decisions in meetings
- when addressing problems, ensure that the facts are established to investigate and, whenever possible, address the cause rather than the effect
- take special care when addressing 'people problems' in meetings – especially if those under discussion are not present or they are in a minority
- when making decisions, always consider the

positive and negative implications of any possible decision – before implementing it

• recording progress – as it is made – will help a meeting (and its structure) stay on track.

———————————————————————

9
Sell the success

Make sure that **everyone** believes that real progress has been made as a result of their attendance.

This can still be true even if the desired outcome was not achieved. For example, in Chapter 8 we talked about the decision process involved in selecting a supplier for a computer system. Suppose none of the selected suppliers were chosen – does that mean the meeting failed in its purpose? I would say it succeeded because had we chosen the 'best of a bad bunch' of suppliers, we might have fulfilled the meeting's goal but singularly failed to deliver a sound decision for the organization. So we have success – albeit we need more research and another meeting to find the *right* supplier.

Was it worth it?

If we take the cost of the participants' salaries for the duration of the meeting (and their traveling and preparation time), add any travelling expenses and location costs, the cost of a meeting can be quite considerable. And you could also consider what has not been earned by participants by being in a meeting rather than at their place of work – the sales call that was missed causing the loss of substantial profit.

So we have a key question to answer:

> **Did the meeting put back into the organizational coffers that which has been spent?**

But don't disregard the soft benefits (in Chapter 1). Since it is difficult to do this in monetary terms, we should also consider the following:

What do the participants think?

Against the declared purpose of the meeting:

- were their expectations met or exceeded? If not, why not? How useful was the meeting and why?
- did anything not happen which was expected to happen?
- did anything undesirable happen? If so, why and how can it be avoided in the future?
- should the meeting start again, how would they prefer it to differ – if at all?

- did everyone attend who should have? Did some attend who needn't?

- was everyone adequately prepared – if not, why not?

- what are the learning points for future meetings?

This can be a group evaluation, although more might be gained from soliciting individual feedback.

A thank you

Whatever you feel inside, always thank everyone for their attendance and contribution. Even if you want to be the first one out of the room – which the chairperson should never be!

Follow up meetings

Most importantly:

> Learn from the feedback of previous meetings – continuous improvement is the goal.

Once we have recognized success, identified how any future meeting should be different (if appropriate) and thanked everyone, it is a golden opportunity to:

> Arrange a follow-up meeting but only if it is genuinely necessary!

Before scheduling any further meeting, ensure that there is a genuine and agreed purpose for it. And how would you determine whether or not a meeting is necessary? Simple, go back to Chapter 1!

Close the meeting

Now, you can declare the meeting over – and remember:

> Finish on time – yet finishing early will usually be well received!

Distributions – minutes or action points?

Now a record of the meeting should be produced, checked by the chairperson and distributed to all participants (and perhaps others). But how much should be recorded during a meeting? Should there be minutes or a set of action points?

I favour action points – they are to the point and make it clear who is to do what by when. I find minutes to be long-winded documents and I never get round to reading them.

There are times, however, when minutes are necessary – perhaps when required by constitutional rules. And they can be helpful to those who didn't attend the meeting – but if their knowledge/input was so important, why did the meeting take place without them?

Follow up

This is crucial:

> Meetings are pointless unless there is follow up. If it doesn't happen, no one should bother going in the first place!

So someone should always ensure that what was agreed and/or promised in a meeting is followed up after the meeting has closed.

In summary

- help everyone to recognize that a meeting has been successful and worthwhile

- find out what the participants thought of the meeting – there may be learning points for the future

- thank everyone for their contribution

- only schedule a further meeting, if one is genuinely required and the purpose is clearly identified

- close the meeting on time, if not early

- all meetings should be followed up with either action points (preferred) or minutes

- if there is no follow through to a meeting, there has been no point in having a meeting.

Enjoy your meetings!

Thank you for reading the Easy Step by Step Guide to Fewer, Shorter, Better Meetings.